Vegetarian

igloo

Published by Igloo Books Ltd
Cottage Farm
Sywell
NN6 0BJ
www.igloo-books.com

10 9 8 7 6 5 4 3 2 1

ISBN: 978 1 84852 725 6

Project Managed by R&R Publications Marketing Pty Ltd

Food Photography: R&R Photostudio (www.rrphotostudio.com.au)
Recipe Development: R&R Test Kitchen

Front cover photograph © Stockfood/Andreas Thumm

Printed in and manufactured in China

Contents

Lentil and Rice Pilaf

Preparation 4 mins **Cooking** 30 mins **Calories** 473

1 cup long-grain rice
200g (7oz) green lentils
3 tbsps vegetable oil
2 tsps garam masala
1 tsp ground cumin
1 tsp ground cilantro
3 onions, sliced

1 Bring a large saucepan of water to the boil. Add rice and lentils, reduce heat and simmer for 15 minutes or until they're tender. Drain and set aside.

2 Heat 2 tsps oil in a skillet over a medium heat, add garam masala, cumin and cilantro and cook, stirring, for 2 minutes. Add rice and lentil mixture and cook, stirring, for 4 minutes longer. Remove from heat, set aside and keep warm.

3 Heat remaining oil in a separate skillet over a medium heat, add onions and cook, stirring, for 6 minutes or until onions are soft and golden. Sprinkle onions over pilaf. Serve hot, warm or at room temperature.

Serves 4

Carrot Balls with Spicy Lentils

Preparation 15 mins **Cooking** 50 mins **Calories** 503

125g (4½oz) fresh angel hair pasta, cut into small pieces
1 tsp salt
250g (9oz) carrots, grated
½ cup flour
1 tsp ground cumin
1 egg, lightly beaten
oil for shallow-frying

Spicy lentils
30g (2oz) butter
1 onion, chopped
1 clove garlic, crushed
1 fresh red chili, deseeded and chopped
2 tsps garam masala
1 tsp ground turmeric
200g (7oz) green lentils
6 cups water
2 tbsps tomato paste
¼ cup chopped fresh cilantro leaves

1 Cook the pasta in lots of salted boiling water in a large saucepan for 8 minutes or until just firm in the center (al dente). Drain.

2 Place pasta, carrots, flour, cumin and egg in a bowl and mix to combine. Form pasta mixture into small balls, place on a plate lined with plastic wrap and chill for 20–30 minutes. Heat oil in a skillet over a medium heat. Add pasta balls and cook, turning several times, for 4–5 minutes or until firm.

3 To make the spicy lentils, melt butter in a saucepan over a medium heat, add onion, garlic, chili, garam masala and turmeric and cook, stirring, for 5 minutes or until onion is soft.

4 Stir in lentils, water and tomato paste and bring to the boil. Reduce heat and simmer, stirring occasionally, for 35–40 minutes or until lentils are cooked. Stir in cilantro leaves and simmer for 2 minutes. Serve with pasta balls.

Serves 4

Lentil and Pasta Loaf

Preparation 12 mins **Cooking** 55 mins **Calories** 535

75g (2½oz) small pasta shapes

125g (4½oz) brown lentils

2 cups wholewheat breadcrumbs, made from stale bread

1 onion, grated

1 carrot, grated

2 sticks celery, chopped

60g (2oz) pine nuts

¼ cup tomato paste

¼ cup water

2 eggs, lightly beaten

2 tbsps Worcestershire sauce

freshly ground black pepper

1 Preheat the oven to 180°C (350°F), and grease an 11 x 21cm (4 x 8in) loaf tin. Cook the pasta in lots of salted boiling water in a large saucepan for 8 minutes or until just firm in the center (al dente). Drain. Wash and drain lentils.

2 Place pasta, lentils, breadcrumbs, onion, carrot, celery, pine nuts, tomato paste, water, eggs, Worcestershire sauce and black pepper to taste in a bowl, and mix to combine. Spoon mixture into tin and bake for 45 minutes or until loaf is firm.

Serves 4

Lentil Pockets

Preparation 15 mins **Cooking** 1 hr **Calories** 410

180g (6oz) red lentils
10g (⅓oz) butter
1 small onion, chopped
2 cloves garlic, crushed
2 carrots, chopped
1 tomato, chopped
1 tbsp chopped fresh oregano or 1 tsp dried oregano
½ cup water
1 bunch spinach, stalks removed, leaves chopped
1 tbsp lemon juice
4 large pita bread rounds, warmed and cut in half
yogurt to serve

1. Place lentils in a large saucepan, cover with water and bring to the boil. Reduce heat and simmer for 30 minutes or until lentils are tender. Drain and set aside.

2. Melt butter in a large saucepan, add onion and garlic and cook over a medium heat, stirring, for 5 minutes or until onion is soft. Add carrots, tomato, oregano and water and bring to the boil. Reduce heat and simmer for 10 minutes or until carrots are tender.

3. Add spinach, lemon juice and lentils to pan, and simmer for 15 minutes or until mixture reduces and thickens. Spoon mixture into pita bread pockets and serve immediately with yogurt.

Serves 4

Lentil Burgers

Preparation 20 mins **Cooking** 1 hr 20 mins **Calories** 584

½ cup red or brown lentils, well rinsed

1¼ cups vegetable stock

1 tbsp olive oil

½ small onion, diced

1 small carrot, diced

½ tsp pepper

½ tsp soy sauce

¾ cup rolled oats, finely ground

1 small egg

4 bread rolls, split and toasted

100g (4oz) mixed salad leaves

1 tomato, sliced

30g (1oz) snowpea sprouts

Dressing

1 cup natural yogurt

¼ cup chopped fresh mint

¼ cup chopped fresh parley

¼ cup chopped fresh dill

1 Place lentils in a saucepan and cover with water. Bring to the boil, then reduce heat and simmer for 25 minutes or until tender, and drain.

2 Return the lentils to the saucepan with stock, bring to a boil, reduce heat, cover, and simmer for 45 minutes, until water is nearly gone and lentils are very soft, with splitting skins.

3 To make the dressing combine all the ingredients in a bowl, cover and refrigerate.

4 Meanwhile, add half of the oil to a large skillet and fry the onion and carrot for 5 minutes. Mix the lentils, onion, carrot, pepper, and soy sauce in large bowl and mix in the ground oats and egg. Form the mixture firmly into patties while still warm.

5 In a clean skillet, heat the remaining oil and fry burgers for 1–2 minutes per side. Place a dollop of dressing on the bottom of each bread roll, top with salad leaves, the warm burgers, tomato slices and sprouts. Serve immediately.

Serves 4

Warm Lentil Salad with Feta

Preparation 10 mins **Cooking** 15 mins **Calories** 478

6 cups vegetable stock
200g (7oz) yellow lentils
200g (7oz) red lentils
2 tomatoes, diced
2 sticks celery, sliced
½ green pepper, diced
½ red pepper, diced
1 small onion, chopped
200g (7oz) Feta cheese, crumbled

Dressing

¼ tsp ground cilantro
¼ tsp ground turmeric
¼ tsp ground cumin
¼ tsp freshly ground black pepper
1 clove garlic, crushed
3 tbsps cider vinegar
1 tbsp olive oil

1 In a medium-sized pot, add half the stock and the yellow lentils. Bring to the boil and cook for 10 minutes. Drain and set aside. In a separate medium-sized pot, add the remaining stock and red lentils, bring to the boil and cook for 5 minutes. Drain.

2 When both sets of lentils are cooked and drained, combine with tomatoes, celery, peppers and onion in a large salad bowl.

3 To make dressing, place spices, garlic, vinegar and oil in a screwtop jar and shake well to combine. Spoon dressing over salad and toss. Sprinkle with the Feta. Serve immediately.

Serves 4

Spicy Lentil and Vegetable Loaf
Preparation 20 mins **Cooking** 1 hr 35 mins **Calories** 604

1 tbsp olive oil
1 clove garlic, crushed
1 onion, chopped
½ tsp chili powder
½ tsp ground cumin
½ tsp ground cilantro
½ tsp ground turmeric
500g (18oz) red lentils
1 carrot, grated
1 large potato, grated
440g (1lb) canned tomatoes,
undrained and mashed
2 cups vegetable stock
3 egg whites
1½ cups rolled oats
freshly ground black pepper
tomato chutney, to serve
60g (2oz) arugula leaves

1 Preheat the oven to 180°C (350°F) and grease an 11 x 21cm (4 x 8in) loaf tin. Heat oil in a large skillet, add garlic, onion, chili powder, cumin, cilantro and turmeric and cook for 4–5 minutes or until onion is soft.

2 Add lentils, carrot, potato, tomatoes and stock and bring to the boil. Reduce heat, cover and simmer for 30 minutes or until lentils are tender. Remove pan from heat and set aside to cool slightly.

3 Place egg whites in a bowl and beat until stiff peaks form. Fold egg whites into lentil mixture.

4 Stir rolled oats into lentil mixture and season to taste with black pepper. Spoon into tin and bake for 1 hour. Serve with tomato chutney and arugula.

Serves 4

Vegetable and Lentil Curry

Preparation 20 mins   **Cooking** 40 mins   **Calories** 320

1 tbsp olive oil

1 onion, sliced

1 clove garlic, crushed

1 tsp ground cumin

1 tsp ground cilantro

1 tsp ground turmeric

2 carrots, sliced

100g (4oz) red lentils

440g (1lb) canned tomatoes, undrained and mashed

2½ cups vegetable stock

1 tsp chili sauce

500g (18oz) pumpkin or potatoes, cut into small cubes

½ head cauliflower, cut into florets

2 tbsps blanched almonds, roughly chopped

freshly ground black pepper

4 tbsps natural yogurt

4 sprigs cilantro leaves, to garnish

1 Heat oil in a large saucepan, add onion, garlic, cumin, cilantro, turmeric and carrots and cook for 5 minutes or until onion is soft.

2 Stir in lentils, tomatoes and stock and bring to the boil. Reduce heat, cover and simmer for 15 minutes.

3 Add chili sauce, pumpkin or potato and cauliflower and cook for 15–20 minutes longer or until pumpkin or potato is tender. Stir in almonds and black pepper to taste. To serve, ladle curry into bowls, top with a spoonful of yogurt and garnish with a sprig of cilantro.

Serves 4

Variation: You could use broccoli instead of cauliflower.

Lentil Fritters with Chili Yogurt
Preparation 12 mins **Cooking** 15 mins **Calories** 500

125g (4½oz) red lentils, cooked

4 scallions, chopped

1 carrot, grated

2 zucchini, grated

½ cup besan flour

2 tbsps chopped fresh cilantro

1 tsp cumin seeds

2 eggs, lightly beaten

¼ cup milk

oil for shallow-frying

Chili Yogurt

1 cup natural yogurt

1 fresh red chili, finely chopped

1 fresh green chili, finely chopped

1 tsp ground cumin

1 Place lentils, scallions, carrot, zucchini, flour, cilantro and cumin seeds in a bowl and mix to combine. Add eggs and milk and mix well.

2 To make chili yogurt, combine yogurt, red and green chilies and cumin in a bowl.

3 Heat 5cm (2in) oil in a frying pan until a cube of bread dropped in browns in 50 seconds. Add tbsps of lentil mixture to pan and cook for 3 minutes each side or until golden. Drain on absorbent paper. Repeat to use remaining mixture. Serve fritters with chili yogurt.

Note: Besan flour is made from milled chickpeas.

Makes 20

Lentils with Pappadums

Preparation 15 mins **Cooking** 40 mins **Calories** 319

3 cups water
2 cups yellow lentils, rinsed
salt
2 tsps finely chopped fresh ginger
2 tbsps vegetable oil
½ tsp ground turmeric
2 onions, thinly sliced
¼ tsp paprika
¼ tsp mango powder
¼ tsp ground cumin
½ cup chopped fresh cilantro leaves
12 pappadums

1 Place water in a large saucepan, add lentils, salt to taste, ginger, 1 tbsp oil and turmeric and cook, partially covered, over a medium heat for 25 minutes. Beat with a hand beater, then reduce heat to the lowest possible setting and simmer for 10 minutes.

2 Heat remaining oil in a small skillet, add onions and cook, stirring frequently, for 5 minutes or until onions are soft and golden.

3 Combine paprika, mango powder and cumin. To serve, spoon lentil mixture into a deep serving dish, top with onions and sprinkle with spice mixture and fresh cilantro. Alternatively, press lentil mixture into a mould, then turn onto a serving plate. Serve with pappadums.

Serves 4

Bean and Tofu Curry
Preparation 10 mins **Cooking** 25 mins **Calories** 338

1 onion, sliced

2cm (¾in) piece fresh ginger, finely grated

½ tbsp mild curry paste

1 tsp ground cinnamon

2 x 440g (1lb) canned peeled tomatoes, mashed

¾ cup vegetable stock

440g (1lb) canned kidney beans, rinsed and drained

400g (14oz) canned butter beans, rinsed and drained

440g (1lb) canned chickpeas, rinsed and drained

300g (11oz) fried tofu, chopped

80g (3oz) chopped roasted peanuts

120g (4oz) green beans, halved

1 In a non-stick saucepan over a medium heat, add onions, ginger, curry paste and cinnamon and cook for 3 minutes, stirring constantly to release the moisture from the onion.

2 Add tomatoes and stock to pan, bring to the boil, then reduce heat and simmer for 5 minutes. Add kidney and butter beans and chickpeas, and simmer for 8 minutes longer.

3 Stir in tofu, peanuts and green beans, reduce heat to low and simmer gently for 5 minutes or until heated through.

Serves 6

Chickpea and Tomato Curry

Preparation 10 mins **Cooking** 20 mins **Calories** 216

1 tbsp vegetable oil

1 clove garlic, crushed

3cm (1in) piece fresh ginger, finely grated

1 onion, chopped

1 tbsp ground cumin

1 tbsp ground cilantro

1 tbsp red curry paste

440g (1lb) canned tomatoes, undrained and mashed

440g (1lb) canned chickpeas, rinsed and drained

125g (4½oz) mushrooms, halved

½ cup fresh cilantro leaves, plus extra to garnish

¼ cup chopped mint leaves

freshly ground black pepper

1 Heat oil in a large saucepan over a medium heat, add garlic, ginger and onion and cook, stirring, for 3 minutes or until onion is golden. Add cumin, cilantro and curry paste and cook for 2 minutes longer.

2 Add tomatoes and chickpeas and bring to the boil. Reduce heat and simmer for 10 minutes.

3 Stir in mushrooms, cilantro and mint, and cook for 2 minutes until curry is heated through. Season to taste with black pepper, sprinkle with cilantro leaves and serve immediately with rice.

Serves 4

Chickpea and Pasta Patties

Preparation 10 mins **Cooking** 20 mins **Calories** 158 per pattie

75g (2½oz) tiny pasta shapes
440g (1lb) canned chickpeas, drained and rinsed
½ cup plain flour
1 onion, chopped
½ cup chopped fresh parsley
1 clove garlic, crushed
1 tsp ground cumin
¼ tsp chili flakes
2 tbsps lemon juice
1 egg, lightly beaten
seasoned flour
oil for shallow-frying

1 Cook the pasta in lots of salted boiling water in a large saucepan for 8 minutes or until just firm in the center (al dente). Drain, set aside and keep warm.

2 Place chickpeas in a bowl and mash. Add pasta, flour, onion, parsley, garlic, cumin, chili flakes, lemon juice and egg and mix to combine. Cover and chill for 1 hour.

3 Divide mixture into 14 portions and shape each into a patty. Roll each patty in seasoned flour to coat.

4 Heat 1cm (⅓in) oil in a skillet over a medium heat and cook patties, in batches, for 3 minutes each side or until golden and heated through. Drain on absorbent paper.

Makes 14 patties

Kebabs with Fava Bean Purée

Preparation 1 hr 15 mins **Cooking** 20 mins **Calories** 182

250g (9oz) cherry tomatoes
155g (5½oz) mushrooms
3 zucchini, cut into thick rounds
1 yellow or green pepper, cut into chunks
250g (9oz) marinated tofu, cut into 2cm (¾in) cubes
1 red pepper, cut into chunks

Marinade

2 tbsps lime or lemon juice
2 tbsps honey
1 tbsp reduced-salt soy sauce
1 tbsp vegetable oil

Fava Bean Purée

250g (9oz) shelled fresh or frozen fava beans
½ cup natural yogurt
1 tbsp chopped fresh thyme or 1 tsp dried thyme
freshly ground black pepper

1 Thread tomatoes, mushrooms, zucchini, yellow or green pepper, tofu and red pepper onto lightly oiled skewers.

2 To make marinade, combine lime or lemon juice, honey, soy sauce and oil. Brush over kebabs and marinate for 1 hour.

3 To make purée, bring a saucepan of water to the boil, add fava beans and cook for 10 minutes or until beans are tender. Drain and cool slightly. Place fava beans, yogurt, thyme, orange zest and black pepper to taste in a blender and process until smooth. Set aside.

4 Cook kebabs under a hot broiler, turning frequently, for 8 minutes or until tender. Serve with purée.

Serves 4

Variation: Any cooked or canned beans can be used in this purée.

Spiced Mung Beans

Preparation 1 hr **Cooking** 30 mins **Calories** 110

400g (14oz) green mung beans

2 tsps vegetable oil

2 large green chilies, deseeded and chopped

2 cloves garlic, crushed

2cm (¾in) piece fresh ginger, grated

1 tbsp yellow mustard seeds

1 tbsp ground cumin

½ cup chopped fresh cilantro

½ cup vegetable stock

½ cup natural yogurt

12 cherry tomatoes, quartered

60g (2oz) alfalfa sprouts

1 Place mung beans in a large heatproof bowl. Boil 1 litre (2 pints) of water and cover mung beans, let stand for 1 hour, then bring a large saucepan of water to the boil. Strain and add mung beans, reduce heat and simmer for 20 minutes or until beans are tender. Drain and set aside.

2 Heat oil in a skillet over a medium heat, add chillies, garlic, ginger, mustard seeds, cumin and cilantro and cook, stirring, for 2 minutes.

3 Add mung beans and stock to pan and cook for 5 minutes longer, until stock is absorbed. Serve in bowls topped with yogurt, cherry tomato pieces and alfalfa.

Serves 4

Butter Bean Hotpot

Preparation 20 mins **Cooking** 50 mins **Calories** 130

250g (9oz) dried butter beans
2 tbsps oil
2 onions, chopped
1 green pepper, chopped
4 tomatoes, chopped
½ cup vegetable stock or water
1 tbsp chopped fresh oregano or 1 tsp dried oregano
2 tsps chili sauce
freshly ground black pepper
125g (4½oz) vintage Cheddar cheese, grated

1 Place beans in a large bowl, cover with water and set aside to soak overnight. Drain beans, place in a saucepan with enough water to cover and bring to the boil. Boil for 10 minutes, then reduce heat and simmer for 1 hour or until beans are tender. Drain and set aside.

2 Heat oil in a saucepan, add onions and pepper and cook, stirring occasionally, for 4–5 minutes or until vegetables are soft. Add tomatoes, stock or water, oregano and chili sauce and bring to the boil. Reduce heat and simmer, uncovered, for 15 minutes or until sauce reduces and thickens. Stir in beans and black pepper to taste.

3 Transfer bean mixture into 4 individual ovenproof dishes, sprinkle with cheese and bake for 20 minutes.

Serves 4

Note: In most recipes that call for dried beans, you can in fact use canned beans if you wish. As canned beans are already cooked, the preparation time of the dish will be much shorter.

Borlotti Bean Frittata

Preparation 10 mins **Cooking** 40 mins **Calories** 432

400g (14oz) can borlotti beans, drained

2 tbsps vegetable oil

1 small onion, sliced

1 medium potato, grated

1 small carrot, grated

2 zucchini, grated

100g (4oz) canned sweetcorn kernels, drained

½ cup chopped fresh parsley

freshly ground black pepper

5 eggs

100g (4oz) tasty cheese, grated

basil leaves, to garnish

1 Preheat the oven to 180°C (350°F). In a large bowl, mash a third of the beans with a fork to make a paste, add remaining beans and set aside.

2 Heat 1 tbsp oil in an ovenproof skillet, add onion and cook over a low heat for 3–4 minutes. Add potato, carrot and zucchini and cook, stirring, for 5 minutes. Remove vegetables from pan and drain on absorbent paper.

3 Add remaining oil to the pan and return the cooked vegetables. Add the sweetcorn, parsley, black pepper, bean mixture and eggs, and gently mix together over the heat to combine.

4 Sprinkle with the cheese and move frittata to the oven. Bake for 30 minutes. Garnish each slice with fresh basil leaves.

Serves 4

Chili Bean Rolls

Preparation 20 mins **Cooking** 20 mins **Calories** 260

150g (5½oz) pre-made puff
pastry
1 egg, lightly beaten

Filling
300g (11oz) canned kidney
beans, rinsed and drained
2 tbsps tomato paste
2 large red chilies, finely diced
30g (1oz) vintage Cheddar
cheese, grated
½ tsp ground cumin
½ tsp ground cilantro

1 Preheat the oven to 180°C (350°F) and grease
   a baking tray. Roll out pastry to 3mm (⅛in)
   thick and cut into eight 10 x 15cm (4 x 5½in)
   rectangles. Set aside.

2 To make filling, place kidney beans, tomato
   paste, chilies, cheese, cumin and cilantro in a
   bowl. Mash lightly to combine.

3 Place a spoonful of filling lengthways down the
   center of each pastry rectangle. Fold ends over
   and roll to encase filling.

4 Place rolls on baking tray, brush with egg and
   bake for 20 minutes or until pastry is puffed and
   golden.

Makes 4

*Note: Serve these tasty rolls with chili sauce and
crisp salad leaves. You can roll the pastries up in
the fresh, crunchy leaves to eat them.*

Spicy Bean and Tofu Nachos

Preparation 5 mins **Cooking** 20 mins **Calories** 705

250g (9oz) corn chips

1 cup pre-made spicy tomato salsa

155g (5½oz) marinated tofu, chopped

440g (1lb) canned kidney beans, rinsed and drained

3 scallions, sliced

1 red pepper, thinly sliced

185g (6oz) vintage Cheddar cheese, grated

1 Preheat the oven to 200°C (400°F). Divide the corn chips between 4 shallow, heatproof bowls. Top each bowl with equal amounts of salsa, tofu, kidney beans, scallions and pepper.

2 Sprinkle with cheese and bake for 20 minutes or until cheese melts and is golden. Serve immediately.

Serves 4

Note: Tofu is very high in protein (approximately 8%), an excellent source of calcium and a good source of iron, phosphorus and B-complex vitamins.

Cabbage Rolls

Preparation 30 mins **Cooking** 40 mins **Calories** 320

8 large cabbage leaves

420g (15oz) canned diced tomato

½ cup orange juice

Filling

⅓ cup rice, cooked

60g (2oz) almonds, chopped

4 scallions, chopped

2 cloves garlic, crushed

1 egg, lightly beaten

60g (2oz) vintage Cheddar cheese, grated

2 fresh red chilies, deseeded and chopped

1 tsp dill seeds

freshly ground black pepper

1 Preheat the oven to 180°C (350°F). Trim thick stalks from cabbage leaves and steam leaves until wilted. Drain and set aside.

2 To make filling, place rice, almonds, scallions, garlic, egg, cheese, chilies, dill seeds and black pepper to taste in a bowl and mix to combine. Divide filling between leaves, fold in the sides and roll up to form neat parcels. Place parcels side by side in a shallow ovenproof dish.

3 Mix orange juice and tomato together, pour over rolls, and cover and bake for 30 minutes.

Serves 4

Stuffed Eggplant

Preparation 20 mins **Cooking** 30 mins **Calories** 340

2 eggplant
4 tbsps salt

Filling
1 tbsp olive oil
1 small onion, chopped
1 clove garlic, crushed
1½ cans tomatoes, drained and chopped
1 tbsp fresh thyme, chopped
1 small egg
¼ cup dried breadcrumbs
45g (2oz) rice, cooked
45g (2oz) Parmesan cheese, grated

1   Preheat the oven to 180°C (350°F) and grease a baking dish. Cut the eggplant in half lengthways and scoop out the center leaving a 2cm (¾in)-thick shell. Sprinkle the inside of each shell with salt, place upside-down on absorbent paper and set aside for 15 minutes.

2   Rinse the eggplant and pat dry with absorbent paper.

3   To make filling, place oil, onion, garlic, tomatoes, thyme, egg, breadcrumbs, rice and Parmesan cheese in a bowl and mix to combine. Divide mixture between eggplant shells, place in the baking dish and bake for 30 minutes.

Serves 4

Note: The filling used in this recipe is also delicious used to stuff other vegetables, such as red or green peppers, zucchini or pumpkin.

Rice Terrine

Preparation 8 mins **Cooking** 45 mins **Calories** 350

10g (⅓oz) butter
1 small onion, chopped
1 cup rice, cooked
⅔ cup milk
2 eggs
½ tsp chili paste
60g (2oz) Parmesan cheese, grated
2 tbsps chopped fresh parsley
freshly ground black pepper
2 red peppers, deseeded and quartered

1 Preheat the oven to 180°C (350°F) and grease an 11 x 21cm (4 x 8in) loaf tin. Melt butter in a skillet, add onion and cook for 4–5 minutes or until soft. Remove pan from heat and set aside.

2 Place rice, milk, eggs, chili paste, Parmesan cheese, parsley, black pepper to taste and cooked onions in a bowl and mix to combine.

3 Spoon a third of the rice mixture into the tin and top with pepper slices. Repeat layers, ending with a layer of rice. Bake for 35–40 minutes. Allow to stand for 10 minutes before turning out and serving.

Serves 4

Note: This terrine is delicious served hot, warm or cold, and leftovers are always a welcome find in a packed lunch.

Rice and Vegetable Patties

Preparation 15 mins **Cooking** 20 mins **Calories** 244

¼ cup brown rice, cooked
¾ cup oat flour
1 small onion, grated
1 clove garlic, crushed
2cm (¾in) piece fresh ginger, grated
120g (4oz) canned sweetcorn, drained
½ carrot, grated
1 small zucchini, grated
2 tbsps pine nuts, toasted
1 tbsp peanut butter
1 tsp soy sauce
1½ tbsps natural yogurt
1 egg white
1¼ cup dried breadcrumbs
1 tbsp olive oil
1 lemon, quartered, to serve

1 Place rice, flour, onion, garlic, ginger, sweetcorn, carrot, zucchini and pine nuts in a bowl and mix to combine. Place peanut butter, soy sauce, yogurt and egg white in a blender and process to combine. Add peanut butter mixture and ½ cup breadcrumbs to rice mixture and mix well.

2 Shape the rice mixture into 12 patties and coat with remaining breadcrumbs. Heat the oil in a non-stick skillet and cook patties for 5 minutes each side or until golden and cooked through. Drain on absorbent paper. Serve with lemon wedges.

Serves 4

Note: Brown rice has only the inedible outer husk removed. The rice retains its bran layer and so is high in vitamin B. Brown rice has a coarser, nuttier texture and flavor than white rice, and is available in both long- and short-grain varieties.

Broccoli and Rice Soufflé

Preparation 20 mins **Cooking** 40 mins **Calories** 172

90g (3oz) broccoli, broken into florets

10g (⅓oz) butter

½ small onion, chopped

1½ tbsps plain flour

165ml (5½ fl oz) milk, heated

¼ tsp ground nutmeg

freshly ground black pepper

2 eggs, separated

50g (2oz) vintage Cheddar cheese, grated

50g (2oz) white rice, cooked

Variation: You can use cauliflower instead of broccoli.

1 Preheat the oven to 180°C (350°C) and grease four ¾ cup soufflé dishes. Steam the broccoli until tender, then drain and refresh under cold, running water. Drain again and set aside.

2 Melt butter in a small saucepan, add the onion and cook for 2 minutes. Stir in flour and cook, stirring constantly, for 2 minutes longer. Remove pan from heat and gradually beat in hot milk. Return pan to heat and cook, stirring constantly, for 5 minutes or until sauce boils and thickens. Stir in nutmeg and black pepper to taste.

3 Beat the egg yolks into sauce, then add the broccoli, cheese and rice and mix well.

4 Place egg whites in a large bowl and beat until stiff peaks form. Stir a quarter of the egg whites into the mixture, then carefully fold in remaining egg whites. Spoon soufflé mixture into soufflé dishes and bake for 25 minutes or until soufflés are puffed and golden. Serve immediately.

Serves 4

Note: For the best volume, have egg whites at room temperature before beating. Egg whites for a soufflé should be beaten until they are stiff but not dry.

Mushroom Risotto

Preparation 5 mins **Cooking** 20 mins **Calories** 440

60g (2oz) butter
1 onion, chopped
2 cloves garlic, crushed
1 cup Arborio rice
100g (4oz) Swiss brown mushrooms
250g (9oz) button mushrooms, sliced
2 cups vegetable stock, heated
3 tbsps chopped fresh parsley
3 tbsps Parmesan cheese, grated
freshly ground black pepper

Variation: You could use asparagus and pepper instead of mushrooms.

1 Melt the butter in a large saucepan, add onion and garlic and cook for 5 minutes or until onion is soft. Add rice and mushrooms and cook, stirring, for 1 minute.

2 Stir in ½ cup of hot stock and cook, stirring constantly, until liquid is absorbed. Repeat until all stock is absorbed. Stir in parsley, Parmesan cheese and black pepper to taste and serve immediately.

Serves 4

Note: Traditional risotto is a great winter warming dish: the combination of mushroooms, cheese and rice in this recipe makes for a substantial meal.

Moulded Tomato Risotto

Preparation 10 mins **Cooking** 35 mins **Calories** 605

2 tbsps olive oil
1 onion, chopped
1½ cups Arborio rice
440g (1lb) canned tomatoes, drained and mashed
1 tbsp tomato paste
3 cups vegetable stock, boiling
60g (2oz) butter
80g (3oz) Parmesan cheese, grated
½ cup fresh basil leaves
freshly ground black pepper

1 Preheat the oven to 200°C (400°F) and grease four moulds. Heat the oil in a large skillet, add onion and cook over a medium heat for 8 minutes or until golden. Stir in the rice and cook for 2 minutes longer.

2 Add tomatoes, tomato paste and stock and cook, stirring frequently, until liquid is absorbed and rice is cooked.

3 Stir in butter, Parmesan cheese and black pepper to taste, and chop three-quarters of the basil leaves (leaving 8 leaves for garnish). Spoon rice mixture into dishes, cover, and bake for 10–15 minutes. Allow to stand 5–10 minutes before turning out and serving. Garnish with the reserved basil leaves.

Serves 4

Vegetable and Bean Risotto

Preparation 10 mins **Cooking** 50 mins **Calories** 276

1 tbsp olive oil
1 tsp mustard seeds
¾ cup Arborio rice
¼ tsp chili powder
1 tsp ground turmeric
1 tsp ground cumin
1 tsp ground cilantro
2 cups vegetable stock
1 small eggplant, cut into small cubes
½ red pepper, deseeded and chopped
300g (11oz) canned butter beans, drained and rinsed
1 cup canned diced tomato
freshly ground black pepper
½ cup fresh cilantro leaves

1 Heat the oil in a large skillet, add mustard seeds, and cook until they begin to pop. Add the rice and cook, stirring constantly, for 4 minutes.

2 Combine chili powder, turmeric, cumin and cilantro with ¼ cup of stock in a small bowl and mix to combine. Stir spice mixture, eggplant, pepper and beans into rice mixture and cook, stirring, for 5 minutes.

3 Add remaining stock and tomato to rice mixture and simmer for 30–40 minutes or until most of the liquid is absorbed and the rice is cooked. Stir in black pepper to taste. Serve immediately, garnished with cilantro leaves.

Serves 4

Variation: You could use any type of beans in this recipe instead of butter beans.

Rainbow Risotto

Preparation 12 mins **Cooking** 30 mins **Calories** 380

1 tbsp vegetable oil
15g (½oz) butter
1 onion, chopped
½ tsp ground turmeric
1 cup Arborio rice
3 cups vegetable stock
250g (9oz) butternut pumpkin, diced
125g (4oz) fresh peas, shelled
1 small red pepper, diced
2 zucchini, diced
freshly ground black pepper

1 Heat the oil and butter in a large saucepan, add onion and turmeric and cook for 2–3 minutes. Stir in rice and stock, bring to the boil, then reduce heat, cover and simmer for 15 minutes or until rice is tender and most of the liquid is absorbed.

2 Steam pumpkin and peas, separately, until tender. Drain and add to rice mixture with pepper and zucchini. Cook for 4–5 minutes longer or until heated through. Season to taste with black pepper and serve immediately.

Serves 4

Hot Chili and Basil Pasta

Preparation 6 mins **Cooking** 12 mins **Calories** 461

320g (11½oz) dried tagliatelle
1 tbsp salt
3 tbsps vegetable oil
315g (11oz) broccoli, broken into florets
1 red pepper, sliced
2 cloves garlic, crushed
2 fresh red chilies, deseeded and chopped
3 tbsps chopped fresh basil
¼ cup soy sauce
¼ cup Chinese rice wine

1 Place the pasta in lots of boiling water in a large saucepan with salt and cook for 8 minutes or until just firm in the center (al dente). Drain, set aside and keep warm.

2 Heat 1 tbsp oil in a skillet over a medium heat, add the broccoli, pepper, garlic and chilies and stir-fry for 2 minutes. Stir in basil, soy sauce, rice wine and remaining oil, bring to the boil, then reduce heat and simmer for 1 minute. Add pasta and toss to combine. Serve immediately.

Note: Serve this dish in shallow pasta plates so that none of the liquid is lost.

Vegetable Ravioli

Preparation 12 mins **Cooking** 40 mins **Calories** 746

15g (½oz) butter
1 leek, sliced
1 clove garlic, crushed
120g (4oz) fresh peas, shelled
2 carrots, chopped
3 cups vegetable stock
¼ cup heavy cream
¼ cup fresh dill, chopped, plus extra to garnish
pinch ground nutmeg
freshly ground black pepper
550g (20oz) pre-made cheese and spinach ravioli
1 tbsp salt
100g (4oz) Parmesan cheese, shaved

1 Melt the butter in a saucepan over a medium heat, add leek and garlic and cook, stirring, for 5 minutes or until leek is soft. Add peas, carrots and stock and bring to the boil. Reduce heat and simmer for 20 minutes or until vegetables are cooked and liquid reduces. Set aside to cool slightly.

2 Place mixture into a blender and process to a purée. Return sauce to a clean saucepan and stir in cream, dill, nutmeg and black pepper to taste. Simmer for 3–4 minutes, or until sauce is heated.

3 Meanwhile, place the pasta in lots of boiling water in a large saucepan with salt and cook for 8 minutes or until just firm in the center (al dente). Drain well and place in a serving bowl. Spoon sauce over pasta, toss to combine and scatter with Parmesan cheese and extra dill.

Serves 4

Orecchiette with Mushrooms

Preparation 10 mins **Cooking** 25 mins **Calories** 763

375g (13oz) orecchiette
1 tbsp salt
30g (1oz) butter
125g (4½oz) mushrooms, sliced
1 onion, thinly sliced
1 clove garlic, crushed
1 tbsp ground paprika
½ cup white wine
2 tbsps tomato paste
1¼ cups sour cream
¼ cup chopped fresh parsley, plus extra to garnish
freshly ground black pepper

1 Place the pasta in lots of boiling water in a large saucepan with salt and cook for 8 minutes or until just firm in the center (al dente). Drain, set aside and keep warm.

2 Melt butter in a saucepan over a medium heat, add mushrooms, onion and garlic and cook, stirring occasionally, for 5 minutes or until onions and mushrooms are soft.

3 Stir in paprika, wine and tomato paste, and simmer for 5 minutes. Remove pan from heat, stir in sour cream and parsley, and cook over a low heat for 2 minutes. Season to taste with black pepper. Add the pasta to the sauce, gently toss to coat and cook for a further 2 minutes. Garnish with extra parsley leaves.

Serves 4

Asparagus and Pasta Quiche

Preparation 15 mins **Cooking** 55 mins **Calories** 824

90g (3oz) small pasta shapes
1 tbsp salt
2 sheets pre-made shortcrust pastry
125g (4½oz) Gruyère cheese, thinly sliced
350g (12oz) canned asparagus tips, well drained
3 small eggs
1 cup heavy cream
pinch grated nutmeg
freshly ground black pepper

1 Place the pasta in lots of boiling water in a large saucepan with salt, and cook for 8 minutes or until just firm in the center (al dente). Drain, set aside and keep warm.

2 Preheat the oven to 180°C (350°F). Roll out the pastry to 5mm thick and use it to line a 20cm (8in) springform tin. Prick the base and sides of the pastry case with a fork, line with non-stick baking paper and fill with uncooked rice. Bake for 15 minutes or until pastry is lightly browned. Remove paper and rice and set pastry case aside to cool.

3 Arrange the cheese over the pastry base, then top with asparagus and pasta.

4 Place eggs, cream, nutmeg and black pepper to taste in a bowl and beat to combine. Carefully pour egg mixture into pastry case and bake for 30 minutes, until filling is firm. Serve hot, warm or cold.

Serves 4

Shell Noodles with Vegetables

Preparation 5 mins **Cooking** 12 mins **Calories** 657

300g (11oz) large shell pasta
1 tbsp salt
300g (11oz) broccoli, broken into florets
220g (8oz) cauliflower, broken into florets
120g (4oz) butter
30g (1oz) pine nuts
30g (1oz) slivered almonds
¼ cup chopped fresh parsley
3 cloves garlic, crushed
1 fresh red chili, deseeded and diced
¼ cup coarse breadcrumbs made from stale bread

1 Place the pasta in lots of boiling water in a large saucepan with salt, and cook for 8 minutes or until just firm in the center (al dente). Drain, set aside and keep warm.

2 Steam broccoli and cauliflower until the broccoli just changes color. Drain, set aside and keep warm.

3 Melt the butter in a skillet over a medium heat, then add pine nuts, almonds, parsley, garlic and chili and cook, stirring, for 2 minutes or until nuts are golden. Add cauliflower and broccoli and toss well to coat with butter mixture. Add breadcrumbs and mix quickly. Spoon vegetable mixture over pasta and toss to combine. Serve immediately.

Serves 4

Penne with Chili and Tomato

Preparation 12 mins **Cooking** 30 mins **Calories** 343

320g (11½oz) penne
1 tbsp salt
¼ cup olive oil
1 large eggplant, cut into small cubes
1 onion, sliced
1 red pepper, chopped
2 fresh red chilies, deseeded and diced
2 cloves garlic, crushed
625g (1⅓lb) ripe tomatoes, peeled, deseeded and chopped
1 tbsp tomato paste
½ cup chopped fresh parsley

1 Place the pasta in lots of boiling water in a large saucepan with salt, and cook for 8 minutes or until just firm in the center (al dente). Drain, set aside and keep warm.

2 Heat 2 tbsps oil in a skillet over a medium heat, add the eggplant and cook, stirring, for 5 minutes. Remove from the pan and drain on absorbent paper.

3 Heat remaining oil in the pan, add onion, pepper, chilies and garlic and cook, stirring, for 5 minutes or until onion softens. Stir in tomatoes, water, tomato paste and eggplant, and simmer for 10 minutes. Spoon sauce over pasta and sprinkle with parsley.

Serves 4

Variation: For a complete meal, serve this robust dish with a tossed green salad and crusty bread.

Spinach Macaroni Cheese

Preparation 8 mins **Cooking** 45 mins **Calories** 978

400g (14oz) pasta shells
1 tbsp salt
½ bunch spinach, chopped

Sauce
50g (2oz) butter
1½ tbsps flour
2⅓ cups milk
100g (4oz) Gruyère cheese, grated
50g (2oz) vintage Cheddar cheese, grated
freshly ground black pepper

Topping
¾ cup dried breadcrumbs
50g (2oz) butter, melted
50g (2oz) Parmesan cheese, grated

1 Place the pasta in lots of boiling water in a large saucepan with salt, and cook for 6 minutes. Drain, set aside.

2 Meanwhile, microwave the spinach in a greased ovenproof dish until just wilted. Stir. Cook for 1 more minute, then cool slightly and squeeze out any excess liquid. Add pasta to spinach and toss to combine.

3 To make sauce, melt butter in a saucepan over a medium heat, stir in flour and cook, stirring, for 1 minute. Remove pan from heat, beat in milk, then cook, stirring, for 5 minutes or until sauce boils and thickens. Stir in cheeses and black pepper to taste. Pour over pasta.

4 To make topping, combine breadcrumbs, butter and Parmesan cheese and sprinkle over pasta. Bake for 20–30 minutes or until sauce is hot and bubbling and top is golden.

Serves 4

Spirelli with Tomato and Basil

Preparation 5 mins **Cooking** 30 mins **Calories** 424

320g (11½oz) spirelli
1 tbsp salt
20g (1oz) butter
1 tbsp olive oil
1 onion, chopped
125g (4oz) mushrooms, sliced
2 x 440g (1lb) canned tomatoes, undrained and mashed
¼ cup fresh basil leaves
freshly ground black pepper

1 Place the pasta in lots of boiling water in a large saucepan with salt, and cook for 8 minutes or until just firm in the center (al dente). Drain, set aside and keep warm.

2 Heat the butter and oil in a skillet over a medium heat, add the onion and mushrooms and cook, stirring occasionally, for 5 minutes or until onion is soft. Add the tomatoes, most of the basil and black pepper to taste, and simmer, stirring occasionally, for 15 minutes or until sauce reduces and thickens.

3 Spoon the sauce over the pasta and garnish with remaining basil.

Serves 4

Apple and Watercress Salad

Preparation 6 mins Calories 66

2 green apples, cored and cut into wedges

1 bunch watercress, picked into sprigs

½ red onion, sliced

3 tbsps snipped fresh chives

4 tbsps pre-made French dressing

Variation: You can use fresh pears instead of apples.

1 Place apples, watercress, onion and chives in a large bowl and toss gently to combine.

2 Drizzle dressing over salad.

Note: Watercress has a peppery taste and has long been used as both a food and a medicine. It's an excellent salad vegetable, whether used by itself or combined with other milder greens. Remember to always wash salad vegetables before using; and it's best to do the washing as close to serving as possible.

Spiced Broccoli Pilaf

Preparation 8 mins **Cooking** 15 mins **Calories** 540

40g (2oz) butter
1 small onion, chopped
1 clove garlic, crushed
½ tbsp cumin seeds
1 cinnamon stick
2 bay leaves
½ tsp ground cardamom
120g (4oz) broccoli, broken into small florets
⅓ cup vegetable stock
1 cup basmati rice, cooked
125g (4½oz) cashews, roasted
2 oranges, segmented

1 Melt the butter in a large skillet, add the onion, and cook for 4–5 minutes or until onion is soft. Stir in garlic, cumin seeds, cinnamon, bay leaves and cardamom and cook for 1 minute.

2 Add broccoli and stock, cover and cook for 5 minutes or until broccoli is tender.

3 Stir in the rice, cashews and oranges and cook for 5 minutes longer or until heated through.

Note: Pilau, pilaf, pilao and pilaw are all the same sort of rice dish – it just depends what country you're in. The dish consists of rice and spices cooked in stock. It's common throughout India and the Middle East, and makes a delicious light meal or accompaniment.

Serves 4

Vegetable Couscous

Preparation 15 mins   **Cooking** 45 mins   **Calories** 720

1½ cups couscous
1½ cups water
4 tbsps olive oil
2 onions, chopped
1 small eggplant, diced
380g (13oz) pumpkin, diced
1 carrot, diced
1 tsp chili paste
2 tomatoes, chopped
2 tbsps tomato purée
1 zucchini, diced
1 cup vegetable stock
40g (2oz) golden raisins
440g (1lb) canned chickpeas, drained
½ cup chopped fresh flat leaf parsley, plus extra to garnish

1 Place couscous and water in a large bowl and set aside to soak for 15 minutes or until water is absorbed. Heat the oil in a large saucepan, add onions, eggplant, pumpkin and carrots, and cook, stirring, for 5 minutes. Stir in chili paste, tomatoes, tomato purée, zucchini and stock and bring to the boil, reduce heat to a simmer. Add the golden raisins and chickpeas, cook for a further 20 minutes.

2 Meanwhile, line a large steamer with a muslin cloth. Steam couscous, covered, for 20 minutes. Remove lid carefully, fluff up the couscous with a fork, cover and steam for 20 minutes longer.

3 Divide couscous between individual serving dishes and top with the vegetable mixture. Garnish with parsley.

Serves 4

Note: Originating from Morocco, couscous is often thought of as a type of grain – in fact, it's a pasta made from durum wheat. However, it's cooked and used in the same way as a grain.

Rose-Scented Saffron Rice

Preparation 4 mins **Cooking** 35 mins **Calories** 577

400g (14oz) basmati rice, washed

50g (2oz) butter

1 small onion, chopped

½ tsp mixed spice

50g (2oz) golden raisins

½ tsp powdered saffron

1 tsp rose water

5 cups vegetable stock

50g (2oz) blanched almonds, toasted

Variation: you can use currants and almonds instead of golden raisins and roasted peanuts.

1 Place the rice in a large bowl, cover with cold water and set aside to stand for 30 minutes.

2 Heat the butter in a large heavy-based skillet over a medium heat, add the onion, and cook for 5 minutes or until soft. Increase the heat, stir in the mixed spice and raisins and cook for 1 minute longer. Remove pan from heat, set aside and keep warm.

3 Place saffron and rose water in a cup and mix. Place stock and half a tsp of rose water mixture in a large saucepan and bring to the boil. Drain rice, add to pan and bring back to the boil, stirring occasionally. Reduce heat, cover and simmer for 15 minutes.

4 Remove pan from heat, cover and set aside to stand for 5 minutes. To serve, sprinkle with remaining rose water mixture and top with almonds.

Serves 4

Pesto Vegetable Slaw

Preparation 5 mins **Cooking** 2 mins **Calories** 225

1 small head broccoli, broken into florets

250g (9oz) savoy cabbage, shredded

1 large carrot, cut into strips

4 scallions, chopped

1 stick celery, cut into strips

1 red pepper, cut into strips

Dressing

90g (3oz) fresh basil leaves

1 clove garlic, crushed

2 tbsps pine nuts, toasted

2 tbsps Parmesan cheese, grated

4 tbsps natural yogurt

4 tbsp hummus

freshly ground black pepper

1 Steam the broccoli until it just changes color. Drain, refresh under cold running water and drain again.

2 Place broccoli, cabbage, carrot, scallions, celery and pepper in a bowl. Toss gently, cover and refrigerate.

3 To make dressing, place basil, garlic, pine nuts, Parmesan cheese, yogurt, hummus and black pepper to taste in a blender and process until smooth. Just prior to serving, spoon dressing over slaw and toss to combine.

Serves 4

Crunchy Split Peas

Preparation 5 mins **Cooking** 10 mins **Calories** 120

100g (4oz) yellow split peas
oil for deep-frying
¼ tsp chili powder
½ tsp ground cilantro
pinch ground cinnamon
pinch ground cloves
1 tsp salt

1 Place split peas in a large bowl, cover with water, and set aside to soak overnight. Rinse peas under cold running water and drain thoroughly. Set aside for at least 30 minutes, then spread out on absorbent paper to dry.

2 Heat 5cm (2in) oil in a skillet and cook split peas in batches until golden. Using a slotted spoon, remove peas and drain on absorbent paper.

3 Transfer cooked peas to a dish, sprinkle with chili powder, cilantro, cinnamon, cloves and salt and toss to coat. Allow peas to cool. Store in an airtight container.

Serves 4

Note: Take care when frying the peas, as even when completely dry they tend to cause the oil to bubble to the top of the pan. These spicy peas are delicious as a snack or pre-dinner nibble with drinks.

Pickled Tomato and Beans

Preparation 4 mins **Cooking** 10 mins **Calories** 172

2 tbsps olive oil

1 clove garlic, crushed

1 tbsp chopped fresh basil

315g (11oz) canned three-bean mix, drained and rinsed

250g (9oz) cherry tomatoes, halved

1 tbsp white vinegar

½ tsp sugar

1 Heat oil in a large skillet, add garlic and basil and cook for 1 minute. Stir in beans and tomatoes, cover and cook for 5–6 minutes.

2 Add vinegar and sugar and cook for 2 minutes longer or until heated through. Serve immediately.

Serves 4

Note: This recipe uses canned three-bean mix, which is a mixture of butter beans, kidney beans and lima beans. Any canned mixed beans can be used.

Fruit and Nut Salad

Preparation 8 mins **Calories** 176

2 red apples, chopped
2 sticks celery, sliced
250g (9oz) strawberries, halved
3 tbsps golden raisins
60g (2oz) chopped pecans

Dressing
2 tsps finely chopped fresh mint
3 tbsps low-fat natural yogurt
2 tbsps lemon juice
freshly ground black pepper

1 Place apples, celery, strawberries, raisins and pecans in a salad bowl.

2 To make dressing, place mint, yogurt, lemon juice and black pepper to taste in a bowl and stir to combine.

3 Spoon dressing over salad and toss to combine. Cover and refrigerate until required.

Serves 4

Index